Managing Projects

Pocket Mentor Series

The *Pocket Mentor* Series offers immediate solutions to common challenges managers face on the job every day. Each book in the series is packed with handy tools, self-tests, and real-life examples to help you identify your strengths and weaknesses and hone critical skills. Whether you're at your desk, in a meeting, or on the road, these portable guides enable you to tackle the daily demands of your work with greater speed, savvy, and effectiveness.

Books in the series:
Leading Teams
Running Meetings
Managing Time
Managing Projects

Managing Projects

Expert Solutions
to Everyday Challenges

Harvard Business School Publishing

Boston, Massachusetts

No part of this publication may be reproduced, stored in or introduced into a re-trieval system, or transmitted, in any form, or by any means (electronic, mechanical, photocopying, recording, or otherwise), without the prior permission of the pub-lisher. Requests for permission should be directed to permissions@hbsp.harvard.edu, or mailed to Permissions, Harvard Business School Publishing, 60 Harvard Way, Boston, Massachusetts 02163.

Library of Congress Cataloging-in-Publication Data

Pocket mentor : managing projects.
     p. cm. — (Pocket mentor series)
  Includes bibliographical references.
  ISBN 1-4221-0187-8
  1. Project management. 2. Title: Managing projects. III. Series.
  HD69.P75P623 2006
  658.4'04—dc22   2005037981

The paper used in this publication meets the requirements of the American National Standard for Permanence of Paper for Publications and Documents in Libraries and Archives Z39.48-1992.

Contents

How to Get the Project Going   29

The build-up phase of a project includes assembling your team, setting the schedule, and developing the budget.

How to Manage the Project   51

Moving forward on the critical path brings a satisfying sense of making progress despite those tedious details. The key to success at this stage is to monitor progress at every step.

How to Manage the Problems   63

Ideas for handling those inevitable problems that every project manager faces.

How to Handle End Matters 73

Wrapping up a project is the time to look back and assess how the project went. What can be learned from these experiences that can improve the process of future projects?

Perform a post-project evaluation 75

Develop a useful final report 75

Enjoy the satisfaction of a job well done 78

Tips and Tools 79

Tools for Project Management 81

Worksheets to help you to plan and manage a project.

Test Yourself 87

A helpful review of concepts presented in this guide. Take it before and after you've read through the guide to see how much you've learned.

To Learn More 93

Further titles of articles and books if you want to go more deeply into the topic.

Sources for Project Management 99

Notes 101

For you to use as ideas come to mind.

Mentor's Message: Exploring Project Management

Project management is a mass of contradictions. You have to create a comprehensive and detailed plan but at the same time be flexible enough to deal with the unexpected. You have to keep the big-picture view—focused on that final goal—while taking care of the small but critical details that keep everything on track. And you need the compassion and energy to inspire your team and the courage to challenge your supervisor when necessary.

As a project manager, you'll need people skills, communications skills, planning skills, vision, and common sense. Luckily, you probably already possess some or all of the skills you need to manage your next project. And even if you think you've never run a project before, chances are you have.

If you've worked in a very project-driven area such as product development, architecture, or video production, you are accustomed to working on projects even if you've never run one. You've met deadlines and stayed within budgets. You understand how to adapt to unexpected problems and events. You have the skills you need to be a team player, and you're probably very aware of the pitfalls to be avoided.

If you work in a support or service area, you probably routinely run projects, too, even if those activities go by another name.

You're running a project if you're:

- a customer-support person preparing for a product upgrade

- a homeowner renovating a kitchen

- a facilities manager supervising a change in the phone system

- a human resources person implementing and communicating a change in benefits

- a coach taking a team on a trip

- a researcher preparing for a grants administrator's audit

- a car owner shopping for a new car

- a bride planning a wedding

This guide will help you build on your strengths, identify and fill in gaps in skills, and give you a clear and organized path to follow—a must for every project manager. It also provides practical tips for dealing with commonly occurring challenges and pitfalls as well as tools you can use in managing projects large and small.

Please join me in exploring project management and in discovering how you can become a better, more confident project manager.

Mary Grace Duffy, Mentor

Mary Grace Duffy, Ed.D., is founding partner of Cambridge Hill Partners, Inc., a management consulting firm, as well as an adjunct faculty member of the Harvard University Extension School and Simmons Graduates School of Management. She has more than thirty years' experience "multi-tasking" as both a line manager and a consultant. She has condensed this expertise into practical techniques for managing tasks and people, planning and decision making, and moving complex projects through to completion.

Project Management: The Basics

The Rewards
of Project
Management

Project managers discover different rewards in their work. For some, it's the pleasure of solving a big problem and the acknowledgment of an achievement. For others, the excitement of making something out of nothing is the big payoff. And for others, working with different kinds of people and developing professional relationships provide the deepest satisfaction.

Why bother?

Here, project managers speak openly of their experiences.

The good ... The rewards of managing a project are as varied and exciting as the kinds of projects and the types of people.

"What's rewarding to me is making the client happy—exceeding their expectations and providing value."
   —Beth Chapman, engagement manager

"In the process of the job, it's the people that I hire to work with me. I take great pride in the people that I surround myself with."
   —Jennifer Sargent, film and video producer

"Trying to make something that wasn't there before—to me, that's interesting."
   —Timothy O'Meara, director of new and technical services

The bad . . . The personal rewards may vary from project manager to project manager, but the downside is almost always the same— the annoying details that demand one's constant attention.

"I least like the tedium of the job. You have to know every nut and bolt. You have to read pages and pages of specifications about every single part of the building—every nail, every screw, every gutter, every shingle, and every brick—and the warranties and how it can be used and how it has to be installed. It's like reading the phone book."
—Victor Ortale, project designer/project architect

"There's so much attention to detail, and that's not my favorite. But it is really important because if you don't do it, you will fail. You have to pay attention to the details or everything starts breaking down."
—Beth Chapman

The real . . . Project management is complex and challenging, creative and tedious, a process with unlimited potential and yet predictable patterns.

What Is
a Project?

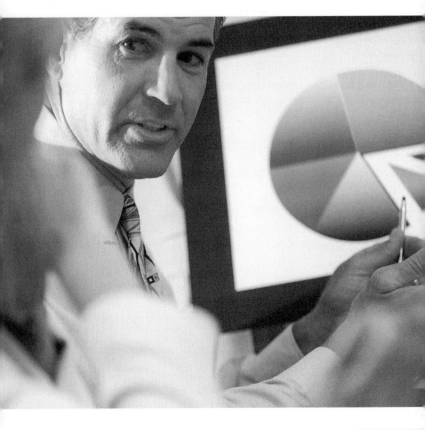

"A project is a problem scheduled to be solved."
—Dr. J. M. Juran

We often hear the words *project* or *project management*, but their meanings may be understood in different ways by different people. For example, *project* can mean a plan or proposal or an undertaking—or it can literally mean a movement forward. So what exactly do we mean when we use these terms?

What is project management?

A project is a job that has to get done. It has an identifiable endpoint. Typically, in business, a project refers to a set of interrelated activities, usually involving a group of people working together on a one-time task for a period of one to eighteen months.

For example, designing a new car is a project. A group of people collaborates on design, building, testing, and modification. Once the new car goes into production, the project ends. The responsibility for producing the car is given to an ongoing department or business unit.

NOTE: When the project ends and ongoing production begins, a manager will still use many of the same project management skills to keep the production process going.

What are the phases of a project's life cycle?

Whether you're in charge of designing a new car, developing a Web site, moving a company, monitoring an external audit, launching a space shuttle, cleaning up a disaster site, updating an information system, or any one of hundreds of other kinds of projects, you'll still go through the same phases.

The life cycle of a typical project comprises four distinct phases:

1. Planning.

2. Build-up.

3. Implementation.

4. Phase-out.

Each phase has its own set of objectives, activities, tools, and skills. The project manager needs to recognize those obejctives, prepare for the activities, and use each set of tools and skills as needed.

Overlapping activities and skills. Even though the phases may have distinct qualities, the major tasks and activities of the four phases often overlap and are iterative. For example, you typically begin the planning phase with a ballpark figure for your budget and an estimated completion date for the project. Once you're in the build-up phase, you begin to define the details of the project plan. These details give you new information, so you return to the planning phase to revise budget and schedule.

Project Phases

Planning	Build-up	Implementation	Phase-Out
Objectives/Goals:			
• Determine the real problem • Identify stakeholders • Define project goals and objectives	• Assemble team • Develop overall plan	• Monitor and control process • Report progress	• Bring project to closure • Identify next steps
Activities:			
• Determine scope, major activities, and tasks • Estimate effort and duration • Assess resource needs • Prepare for tradeoffs	• Develop project schedule • Create critical path • Motivate team • Assign people and resources to tasks • Develop budget • Delegate tasks as needed • Clarify stakeholders' expectations	• Review and approve work-in-process • Deliver project milestones • Manage development process • Communicate progress and problems to stakeholders	• Evaluate performance • Close out project • Debrief lessons learned with team • Create follow-up plan • Review results with stakeholders
Key Skills:			
• Task analysis • Planning • Cost-benefit analysis of options	• Analysis of process • Team building • Delegating • Negotiating • Recruiting and hiring • Communication	• Supervising • Leading and motivating • Communication • Conflict management • Problem solving	• Follow-through • Planning • Communication
Tools:			
• Work Breakdown Structure (WBS) • Skills inventory	• Scheduling tools (CPM, PERT, GANTT)	• Progress report tools	• Project evaluation tools

Returning to the activities and tasks of an earlier phase in this way does not mean you are moving backward; it simply means that you are incorporating new knowledge and information into the overall plan—viewing the big picture.

How to
Plan a Project

Within each phase, there are further predictable elements in the process of managing a project.

For the planning stage, these steps are:

1. Defining the real problem.

2. Identifying the stakeholders.

3. Setting the objectives.

4. Preparing for trade-offs.

5. Defining the activities.

Define the real problem

Before you begin, take time to determine the real problem the project is trying to solve. It's not always so obvious.

Defining the real problem is a critical step. Too often, in the desire to get something done—release a new product or deliver a solution to a perceived problem—you can leap to the solution before completely understanding what the problem is.

EXAMPLE: Asked to develop a new database and data entry system, an IT manager could jump right into it. After all, he's been waiting for the go-ahead to move the system from bleeding edge to leading edge. But will that solve his company's problem? To increase his chance of a successful project, the IT manager needs to go beyond the symptoms of the problem—"*We can't get the data out fast enough*" and "*I have to sift through four different reports just to compile an update on my clients' recent activity*"—to find the underlying problems and needs. Before designing the database, he may ask what type of data is needed, what is going to be done with it, how soon a "fix" is needed, and so on.

Without understanding the real underlying problem, you run the risk of wasting time and money by designing a solution that is either too simplistic, too complicated, too late, or that doesn't do what the users need it to do.

To uncover the real needs of a project, answer these questions:

- What is the perceived need or purpose for what we are trying to do?

- What caused people to see this as a problem that needs solving?

- Who has a stake in the solution or outcome?

- How do the various stakeholders' goals for the project differ?

- What criteria are people going to use to judge this project a success?

STAKEHOLDER *n* **1:** anyone who has a vested interest in the outcome of your project. Contributors, customers, managers, and financial people are all stakeholders; they are the people who will judge the success or failure of the project.

What Would YOU Do?

The Wrong Tool for the Job

Eun Soon's boss reacted immediately to the dismal quarterly revenue results. "*This has to be fixed and it has to be fixed now. No, not now, yesterday! I want a new incentive plan, and I want it on my desk ASAP!*" He always talked like that, wanting things "ASAP" and "last week." As a hotel manager, Eun Soon was excited to be assigned to her first companywide project. But even though she could understand why her boss had focused on a new incentive plan, she knew incentives weren't going to be enough. Most employees wanted to do a good job and serve customers well, but the hotel's internal processes and systems were getting in the way. The company never put enough time into training new recruits, and it showed. And there were problems with the registration system. Incentives weren't going to solve the revenue problem, but how could Eun Soon tell that to her boss? She didn't want to question the project's merits since this was such a big opportunity for her. On the other hand, she did not want to set herself up to fail.

What would YOU do? The mentor will suggest a solution in *What you COULD do.*

Identify the stakeholders

To help you identify all the stakeholders in a project, consider:

- What functions or people might be affected by the project's activities or outcomes?

- Who contributes resources—people, space, time, tools, and money—to the project?

- Who ultimately will use and benefit from the output of your project?

Once you have identified the stakeholders, work with them to spell out exactly what success on the project means for them. It's useful to have them actually sign off on what they expect at the end of the project and what they are willing to contribute to it. Because stakeholders' interests vary, their definitions of success are likely to differ. One of your critical tasks in this phase is to meld stakeholders' expectations into a coherent and manageable set of project objectives.

What if the stakeholders change in the middle of the project? This situation is not unusual. Be prepared not only to respond to the new stakeholder but also to include all the other stakeholders in any decision to redirect the project.

"If a new player is thrown at you, you have to find out what their issues are, how legitimate the issues are, and how you can convince everyone to be reasonable. You say, 'Well, we could go back and rewire the whole building, but up until a week ago you were fine with the way it was, and it was done perfectly to code.' "

—Victor Ortale

Get support from above. Whether you're managing a project in a corporation or working as an independent consultant for a client, it's critical to have the support of the people you're working for.

All too often, a client or person in upper management has a blue-sky view of what can be accomplished, by when, and for how much. They may expect an enormous amount of work to be done within an unrealistic time period, with an unrealistic budget, or with inadequate resources or staff. The requirements and the resources have to line up fairly evenly, or you as the project manager could be setting yourself up for failure.

Often, it takes some renegotiating to bring the requirements into line with the resources, but in an environment of reasonable people, this is usually possible.

Unfortunately, in some organizations, setting unrealistic goals is standard operating procedure. At a certain point, a manager who's constantly put in this position must decide if it's worth the effort. There's a point at which you have to cut your losses and get out—withdraw from the project, ask to be transferred to another area of the company, or even leave the company. The earlier, the better—you should know at this stage whether or not the project has a chance for success.

"The success of the initiative is quantified with measurable goals. In those goals, I highlight the ways in which [the support of] executive management is required for success of the project. If there isn't executive sponsorship, there are times when we won't take the job."
—Beth Chapman

Set project objectives

The success of a project will be defined by how well you meet your objectives. The more explicitly you state your objectives at the outset, the less disagreement there will be at the end about whether you have met them. In the planning phase, however, much is still in flux. Be prepared to revise your objectives as you gather information about what you need to achieve.

When defining an objective, think SMART. In other words, an objective should be

- **S**pecific
- **M**easurable
- **A**ction-oriented
- **R**ealistic
- **T**ime-limited

EXAMPLE: Over the next four months, the health-care benefits task force of the HR department will come up with a new benefits plan. Its SMART objectives are:

1. To survey <**action-oriented**> at least six <**measurable**> providers that meet the department's minimum threshold criteria for service quality.

2. Recommend <**action-oriented**>, at the June <**time-limited**> board of directors' meeting, the three <**specific**> that offer the best and broadest coverage at a cost that is at least 10% <**realistic**> less than the company's current per-employee contribution.

Defining Your Project

Uncover the issues and parameters at the core of your project.

The "Real" Project

What is the perceived need or purpose for what we are trying to do?
We need to migrate Web servers and databases to a new data center.

What caused people to see this as a problem that needed solving?
The present location has reached its capacity and will not allow for anticipated future growth. Additionally, the architecture of the new datacenter is more efficient, robust, and redundant.

What criteria are people going to use to judge this project a success?
- Minimal downtime to both the Web servers and the databases.
- Minimal impact to the Web users.
- Clean restart and test of all crucial processes.
- Outages contained within their work windows.

The Stakeholders

Who has a stake in the solution or outcome?
Webmasters/administrators and database administrators.
Datacenter manager and employees.

How do the various stakeholders' goals for the project differ?
The Web administrators are primarily concerned with Web content and access to Web sites for users. Database administrators are chiefly concerned with database content, access and integrity. Data center personnel want a smooth transition from the old site to the new one.

What functions or people might the project's activities or outcomes affect?
If the Web sites are down, particularly for an extended period of time, there will be a greater-than-anticipated loss of Web traffic.
If the databases do not transition cleanly or if data is lost from the databases, financials could be affected.

Who is going to contribute resources? (People, space, time, tools, money)
Server, Web, and database administrators.
Additional Web and database servers to create "mirrored" sites.
Additional physical space within the new data center.

Skills Required for the Project

Skill Needed	Possible Team Member
1. Server administration	1. Molly
2. Web site administration	2. Rafael
3. Database administration	3. Peter
4. Network technicians	4. Phil, Carmen

Keep in mind the following aspects of the project as you set your objectives:

- **Quality.** Identify quality standards relevant to the project, and determine how to measure and satisfy them.

- **Organization.** Identify project roles, assignments, and relationships, and make sure you have the right people assigned to the project.

- **Communication.** Determine what information each stakeholder needs and how to deliver it.

- **Risk.** Determine the risks likely to affect the project and evaluate possible responses.

Prepare for trade-offs

Time, cost, and quality are the three related variables that most often determine what it is possible for you to achieve. The simple formula is

$$Quality = Time + Cost$$

Change any one of these variables and you change your outcome. Thus, if you shorten the amount of time you have to complete the project, you either have to increase the cost or lower the quality.

EXAMPLE: A large insurance and financial services company wants to develop a software system to support their disability coverage. Software developers work directly with users throughout the process so that the most appropriate trade-offs can be made. Lead software designers meet regularly with nurses, claims analysts, and accountants to discuss functionality, budget, and timelines.

Of course, changes in the equation often occur in the middle of a project. If your time frame for developing a new database management system is suddenly cut in half, you will need either to employ twice the number of people or else be willing to be satisfied with a system that isn't as robust as originally planned.

Remember, however, a lower-quality product is not necessarily a bad thing: the key is to establish a level of quality that meets your needs. So, if the lack of a database system is impairing mission-critical activities, it may be that your stakeholders just need something that works; they may be more concerned about getting it up and running than making sure it has all possible bells and whistles.

Knowing from the start which of these three variables is most important to each of the stakeholders will help you make the changes needed as they occur.

"It's give and take. Everybody understands budgeting. They will be willing to give up functionality in exchange for a reduced budget or speedier delivery. They have a feel for what they have to sacrifice to get something else. Wishful thinking should be suppressed."

—Susanna Erlikh, software development project manager

Deciding how to make trade-offs between time, cost, and quality—this is the stuff of project management. It's your responsibility to keep all stakeholders informed of any changes in your project's objectives—and what the consequences of those changes will be in terms of time, cost, and quality.

"It's intuitive to understand that the larger the project gets, the more complex the interactivity gets. The job of a good project manager is to keep the actual work being done on a granular enough level to reduce the complexity as much as possible."
—Matt Hotle, senior analyst

Define the activities

Many projects fail either because a significant part of the work has been overlooked or because the time and money required to complete it have been grossly underestimated. One tool that many project managers find helpful in planning is the Work Breakdown Structure.

Tip: When to stop subdividing? Stop when you reach the point at which the work will take an amount of time equal to smallest unit of time you want to schedule. Thus, if you want to schedule to the nearest day, break down the work to the point at which each task takes a day to perform.

Tips: Estimating Effort and Duration

- Base estimates on experience, using the average expected time to perform a task.

- Estimates are not guarantees. Don't let them become firm commitments at this phase.

- When presenting estimates to stakeholders, make sure they are aware of all the assumptions and variables built into them.

Use the Work Breakdown Structure. The Work Breakdown Structure (WBS) is a tool for developing estimates, assigning personnel, tracking progress, and showing the scope of project work. The underlying concept is to subdivide a complex activity into smaller tasks, continuing until the activity can no longer be subdivided. At that point, you have defined each task in its smallest—and most manageable—unit.

To create a WBS:

- Ask, "What will have to be done in order to accomplish X?"

- Continue to ask this question until your answer is broken down into components or tasks that cannot be subdivided further.

- Estimate how long it will take to complete each of these tasks and how much each will cost in terms of dollars and person-hours.

Work Breakdown Structure

Develop a Work Breakdown Structure (WBS) to ensure that you do not overlook a significant part of a complex activity or underestimate the time and money needed to complete the work. Use multiple pages as needed.

Describe the overall project:

The overall project will migrate 3 Web servers and 2 databases to a new physical data center. The project requires that 5 new servers be provisioned in the new data center; these servers will mirror the production servers existing in the old data center. The new servers will be built to the same specifications as the old ones, they will run the same application and have the same content. Once implemented, the new equipment will be tested to confirm functionality. The sites will have a cutover and "go live" data. Finally, the old equipment will be decommissioned and reabsorbed into inventory.

Major Task	Level 1 Sub Tasks	Level 2 Sub Tasks	Level 2 Sub Task Duration
Obtain equipment.	Purchase 3 Web servers and 2 databases.	Cut P.O. and order servers.	5 days
	Ship equipment to new datacenter.	Alert data center that equipment is slated for arrival.	2 days
Provision and implement equipment.	Physically install hardware.	Rack and cable new equipment in data center and ensure physical and network connectivity.	2 days
	Load operating systems.	Load base-level operating systems for Web and database servers.	1 days
	Load applications.	Load application level software, including Web server software, database applications, and any required dependencies.	2 days
	Mirror content to new servers.	Copy configurations from production sites, transfer files to new servers, and load appropriately.	3 days
Test equipment.	Test machines.	Ensure network connectivity, as well as Web and database access functionality, and integrity.	2 days
Go live with new equipment.	Cutover to new production site.	Switch Web and database access to new sites.	1 day
	Data and content integrity check.	Run a series of predetermined tests to ensure that data is accurate and that any updates since mirroring have been captured and applied as necessary.	1 day
Test again.	Let sites burn in for 24 hours and check integrity once again.	Run series of tests once more to ensure that updates and logging is functioning correctly.	1 days
Decommission old equipment.	Remove equipment from datacenter.	De-install equipment, erase software and content.	1 day
	Reabsorb equipment for future use.	Ship equipment back to inventory.	1 day

What You COULD Do.

Let's go back to Eun Soon's planning problem.

The mentor suggests this solution:

Eun Soon needs to help her boss articulate the real goals of the project. Given his "ready, fire, aim" style, she will have to act quickly and prepare a presentation of compelling data to support her approach. She can approach her boss, saying, *"I am operating on the assumption that at the end of this project, what you want is a strategy for increasing revenue. You want something that really works. Is that right?"* Once she has agreement on the desired outcome, she can share some data. For example, first, even when used properly, the registration and checkout system is cumbersome and generates customer complaints, and second, the finance office reports an increased number of uncollectible bills because data was not entered properly. Eun Soon can use this information to negotiate an opportunity to fully define the causes of the problem before beginning to invest time, money, and resources in an approach that may not work.

"I'm considered a good planner, but I don't enjoy planning. I do it because after having experienced what happens when you don't plan, I know what the consequences will be. The farther you get into a project, the worse it gets. And, since I hate a mess, I know to plan early."
—Susanna Erlikh

A WBS typically consists of three to six levels of subdivided activities. The more complex the project, the more levels it will have. As a general rule, no project should have more than 20 levels—and only an enormous project would have that many.

Here in the planning phase, don't worry about the sequence in which activities are performed. You will take care of scheduling in the build-up phase. Use the WBS during the planning phase to help you build the framework that you'll fill in once you have a better sense of your staff, budget, and time constraints.

Padding estimates is an acceptable way to reduce risk, but do it openly and communicate your reasons for doing so to the stakeholders. For example, if your estimate is based on receiving certain products within a two-week period, make sure that expectation is clear so that the stakeholders know there is a chance those products may not arrive in time—and let them know what the consequences of a late arrival would be.

The result of thoughtful planning will be a rough estimate of how many people—with what skills—you'll need for the project. You'll also have a good idea of how long the project will take. The plan is the foundation for the build-up phase.

How to Get the Project Going

*"If you drive your project around without a map
or ignore the orientation clues, you are missing the main
features of the project plan. Mark those milestones well."*

—Martin Nemzow, high-tech consultant and author

W ith your plan in place, it's time to get going. In the build-up phase, your high-level plan turns into action. Your time estimates become schedules. Activities are sequenced into a critical path. Cost estimates become budgets. You bring your team together. You gather your resources. You get commitments and you make them.

Thus, the critical steps in the build-up phase include:

1. Assembling your team.

2. Setting the schedule.

3. Developing a budget.

Assemble your team

The build-up phase begins with an assessment of the skills needed for the project. This assessment flows directly from your work on the Work Breakdown Structure during the planning phase, in which you developed your best estimate of the necessary tasks and activities. Depending on this assessment, your current team may not have certain requisite skills, and so you may need to recruit people who have them. Be prepared to fight to bring in people— either temporary workers or employees from within the organization—who have the additional skills the project needs.

"Picking a good team is about picking qualified people who like working in a group. And I like giving people chances, breaking them into new jobs. I see the potential in the people and help them move up the ladder. A lot of people in my position see the potential but they don't want to take the risk. But I'm willing to."
—Jennifer Sargent

In certain cases, a project manager chooses some or all of his team members. Or a project manager may be assigned a team. If your team is assigned, then, as project manager, you need to assess your team members' skills. Make assignments according to the best matches between skill and task. You may need to provide training for people who need additional skills. Don't forget to budget time and money for any training you or your team may need to cover these skill gaps.

"In the old days, maybe you'd have enough people under you that you could do major projects in your own organization, but now you have to go out into the company and select the people in the company who have the right knowledge. You have to use influence. And if you find you don't have the knowledge base in-house, you have to go into the consulting world to get to it."
—Timothy O'Meara,

What Would YOU Do?

Short Circuit

W hen he first launched the company's new public relations program, Brett had enjoyed the constant commotion. It was great to feel the air charged with creative energy. But now, three months into the project, the only electricity was static. Kelly and Joe kept designing speeches and press briefings that didn't seem to fit together. They kept asking him for lists of speakers, and when he asked them to line up the speakers themselves, they said they had too much other work to do. The public relations people were demanding information that Brett didn't have, and worst of all, Brett's boss had just asked if the division head could come and get a progress update. How far along were they? When would they begin to see the results of their efforts? How should Brett know? He was only the guy in charge. What was he doing wrong? And how could he get the project back on track before someone pulled the plug on it?

What would YOU do?

In today's world, it's common to encounter cross-functional teams, teams created by people from several organizations, or teams made up of groups of people who have never worked together before. As the project manager, you need to pull together the right knowledge base, but each team member also has to understand how to manage his part of the project, and have the willingness to work as a group.

Assign people to tasks. If you've built your own team, you've probably already decided who will do what. Or, if you're simply assigned a team, but you have worked with these people before and know them well enough, make the assignments yourself.

But if a new, unfamiliar group is assigned to you, get to know them before assigning people to tasks.

One method of dealing with new team assignments is the following:

1. List all the people who are part of the project team.

2. List all the skills that are required.

3. Talk to each team member about her own skill set.

4. Match people to the skills and tasks required.

This method starts the process of team communication and cohesion. For example, if the project calls for a skill no one on the team possesses, team members may know someone else who does have that skill. Or you can plan to have a team member trained in that skill.

"If you can't build a team and build that trust, then you can't do the job. There has to be synergy and respect. People on a new team coming together don't always know how to work together, but everyone has to be willing, and dedicated to finding a way to do it quick."
—Beth Chapman

Plan a kick-off meeting. Once you've assembled your team, get them involved immediately at a kick-off meeting. Go over the plan and the project's objectives with them in as much detail as possible. Review the proposed schedule.

Be sure to discuss clearly their roles and responsibilities.

- How will they work together?
- Can they all commit to the plan?
- Can they all commit to the schedule?

Encourage people to point out spots where they see problems may occur and where improvements could be made. Take all suggestions seriously—especially in areas where the team members have more experience than you do—and adjust your estimates and activities accordingly.

Set the schedule

It would be nice to be able to say, *"With the resources we have, the project will need this much time."* The reality is that most projects come with fixed beginning and end dates, regardless of available resources. For example, although you would like to get started immediately, the people or materials may not be ready for another two weeks. Scheduling is a universal task. Every project has a schedule, and every project manager must be able to set one.

"Things always take more time than you think they will."
   —Ken Bell, producer

Tips: Working with a Team

- Even if you are familiar with all the parts of the project, chances are you have not worked on them as recently as some of your team members. Listen to those with special experience, knowledge, or skills. If you insist that yours is the only way to do something, you will be cutting yourself off from important sources of experience and wisdom, and the project will suffer.

- Share the "big picture" information with the team. If they truly understand the intent and purpose of the project, they will be better able to contribute and participate.

How to create a project schedule.
Start by looking at a "drop-dead" date—a date that cannot be changed. The date could be a trade show or the delivery of an audit to a regulatory agency. Work backwards from the drop-dead

date to see when deliverables must be ready. If an annual report is due for the shareholder's meeting and you know it takes the printer two weeks, then all the final art and copy for the report must be ready to go to the printer two weeks before the meeting. Working backwards, or "back-chaining" is an excellent way to create a realistic schedule.

Tips: Scheduling a Project

- Know which deadlines are hard and fast and which have some flexibility.

- No task should last longer than four to six weeks. When tasks approach that time frame, they need to be broken down further.

- Don't schedule more detail than you yourself can actually oversee.

- Develop schedules according to what is logically possible. Resource allocation should be done later.

- Record all time segments in the same increments, such as in days or weeks.

- Do not schedule a project so that overtime is needed to meet original target dates; this doesn't leave any flexibility for handling problems that might occur later.

Steps for Creating the Project Schedule

1. Use the Work Breakdown Structure or a similar outline to develop a list of specific activities or tasks.
2. Assign a deliverable to each activity—for instance, "rough draft of survey questions" or "prototype for test market" or "beta version."
3. Use deliverables as a basis for creating a project schedule with realistic milestones and due dates.
4. Identify bottlenecks that could upset the schedule.
5. Determine ways to remove bottlenecks, or build in extra time to get around them.
6. Establish control and communication systems for updating and revising the schedule.
7. Keep everyone—all the stakeholders—involved in and informed of the project's progress and any schedule modifications.

Steps for Developing a Critical Path

1. List all the activities and give a brief description of each.
2. Determine the expected duration of each activity.
3. List the activities that must be completed prior to each activity's start.
4. Draw the critical path diagram. (See page 39.)
5. Compute the earliest start times for each activity.
6. Compute the earliest finish times for each activity.
7. Identify the critical path.
8. Estimate the expected duration of the entire project.

Following the Critical Path Method. The Critical Path Method (CPM) is a tool for scheduling project activities. Using the results of the Work Breakdown Structure (WBS), you can now take those individual activities and plot a sequence of activities from the project's start to finish. Some activities can move along simultaneously, but other activities must be completed before the next ones can begin. The CPM helps you plan for this process.

The *critical* activities are the ones that determine the total project time—those activities that must be completed on time for the project to meet its deadlines. Identifying which activities are critical allows you to allocate your resources most efficiently.

For example, consider a project involving six activities with the following requirements and time expectations:

Activity	Requirement	Time to Complete
A		5 days
B		3 days
C	A and B completed	4 days
D	B completed	7 days
E	A completed	6 days
F	C completed	4 days

The critical path (figure 1) can be diagrammed using circles to indicate the activity.

The diagram tells you that the earliest you can complete the project is in 11 days. You also see that activities A and E are *critical*

FIGURE 1

Critical path diagram

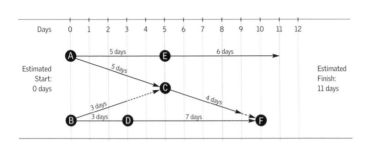

for the project to meet that deadline. Using this information, you may want to readjust your resources and put more toward these critical activities.

Several software programs are available to help you construct more complex versions of the critical path.

Monitoring with the PERT chart. There are two other widely accepted tools for scheduling and monitoring projects—flow charts such as the Performance Evaluation and Review Technique (PERT) and bar charts such as the Gantt chart (see figures 2 and 3).

The PERT chart is similar to the CPM. The CPM's primary purpose is to establish what the critical path is—what the essential tasks are—at the start of the project, so that the project manager can plan carefully for these critical tasks. The PERT chart, on the other hand, shows the progress of each task or the entire project, and is used more as a monitoring tool.

FIGURE 2

Project Phoenix PERT chart

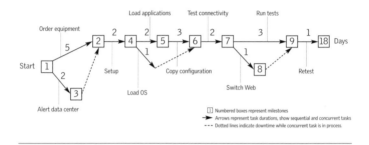

Flow charts, such as PERT charts, show the following:

- when every project task within a phase should begin

- how much time is scheduled for each task (and when it should be complete)

- all tasks in progress at a given time

- all the dependencies between outcomes, tasks, and events

Using the Gantt chart. A Gantt chart illustrates the duration and chronological order of tasks or activities (see figure 3). Unlike a flow chart, however, a Gantt chart does NOT show task dependencies—that is, which task must be completed before another begins.

FIGURE 3

Gantt chart for Project Phoenix

Bar charts, such as Gantt charts, show the following:

- status of project

- estimated project duration

- estimated task duration

- task sequences

"A Gantt chart helps you see the big picture. It can really help people from other divisions and from outside the company see how you do things. I also use a Gantt chart to show clients the high-level milestones, so we can talk about the process, and everyone can see it. It's a very useful tool, but don't let it run the project. Don't ignore opportunities that come up unexpectedly just because they don't fit into the Gantt chart."

—Beth Chapman

Steps for Building a Gantt Chart

The word *building* when creating a Gantt chart is an accurate description of the process. You are constructing the visual framework of the project. Here's how:

1. List phases of project, from first to last, down left side of page.

2. Add time scale across the top or bottom from beginning to deadline.

3. Draw a blank rectangle for phase one from phase start date to estimated completion date.

4. Draw rectangles for each remaining phase; make sure dependent phases start on or after the date that any earlier, dependent phases finish.

5. For independent phases, draw time-estimate rectangles according to preferences of people doing and supervising the work.

6. Adjust phase-time estimates as needed so that the entire project finishes on or before deadline.

7. Add a milestone legend as appropriate.

8. Use graphics to indicate which stakeholder group has responsibility for completing a particular activity.

9. Present the chart to stakeholders and team members for feedback.

10. Adjust as needed

Choosing the scheduling system that's best for you and your project. In all likelihood you will wind up using both bar charts and flow charts at different times. Both these scheduling methods help you visualize what has to be done, how long a particular activity will take, in what order each activity has to happen, and who is responsible for each activity.

Bar charts are very good for showing stakeholders and end users how the project is progressing. Use a flow chart to manage closely and communicate detailed information to supervisors and people doing the work. This is an especially powerful tool in networked computer environments where everyone can keep track of changes to the schedule as they occur.

NOTE: Compare the two scheduling methods

Flow charts (CPM or PERT):

Pro: Allow much greater knowledge of all parts and interdependencies of a project.

Con: Complex and not quickly mastered.

Bar charts (Gantt):

Pros: Simple to construct; easy to read; an effective way to communicate with stakeholders what needs to be done in a given time frame.

Cons: Difficult to assess the impact of a change in one area on the rest of the project; difficult to keep constantly updated as the project gets into full swing.

However, the best method for scheduling a project is the one you are comfortable with and works for you. Don't be lured into using something just because "everyone else does" or because "it's cutting edge."

To assess what method suits you best, use your experience first. Look at the system you use for tracking your own work and see how satisfied you are with it. That may be a guide for you to decide whether to stay with your current system or try some new ones.

Using software for project planning. For complex projects, most project managers use software programs to help with project planning and management. To determine which software is best for you, get as much information about your software options as possible. Check the Internet for information. Get recommendations from other people; compare their work habits against your own to see if it's a good fit. Unless you are already familiar with the software, make sure you can get reliable training and technical support for it.

NOTE: Remember—software is not infallible. It won't be able to check for faulty logic when putting together a schedule. Review the schedule carefully with another team member or stakeholder before finalizing it.

Develop a budget

A budget is the financial blueprint or action plan for the project. It is the translation of plans into measurable quantities that denote the costs of the resources required and anticipated returns over a certain period of time. Not all budgets are the same.

Most project managers have some "wiggle room" in their budgets. However, in some industries (such as grant-sponsored nonprofits), a budget is less flexible than in others. In these cases, the budget is a contract, and money allocated for one line item cannot be spent on another line item without preapproval.

Tips: Selecting Project-Management Software

Any project-planning software should:

- handle development of and changes to Gantt charts and flow charts, including PERT diagrams and calculations of critical paths
- provide on-screen viewing of information before printing
- produce schedule and budgets
- integrate project schedules with a calendar allowing for weekends and holidays
- let you create different scenarios for contingency planning and updating
- warn of overscheduling of individuals and groups

"Once I create a budget and put a limit on how much can be spent, I break it down into categories. I try to stay within that amount in each category. But if I begin to creep over in one category, as long as I come in under in another category—as long as the overall amount is still below when I've actualized—then that's fine."

—Jennifer Sargent

Determine line items. A budget is not only a list of all the costs to execute the project, but also a look at whether the project's benefits justify its costs.

The first question to ask when developing a budget is: *"What is it going to take to actually do the project?"*

To determine a project's costs, break it down into the following categories:

- **Personnel.** This is typically the largest part of your budget. Have you included the costs for both your current employees and any contract workers you may need to add?

- **Travel.** Is everyone onsite, or will employees have to be brought in from other locations?

- **Training.** Does everyone know how to use all the equipment needed to accomplish the project? Do the members of your team possess all the required skills? Will training take place onsite or will it involve travel?

- **Supplies.** In addition to the usual computers, pens, papers, software, and so on, is there any particular or unusual equipment that will be needed?

- **Space.** Do people have to be relocated from their current space? How much room will be required and at what cost?

- **Research.** Will you have to buy studies or data to support this project? How much research will your team have to perform itself? At what cost?

- **Capital expenditures.** What more expensive equipment or technical upgrades will be necessary to do the job? Will any capital expenditures pay for themselves, and how?

- **Overhead.** What is your projected overhead expense? Be sure it is in line with your company's standard overhead percentage.

Once the figures from these standard categories have been entered into the budget, ask yourself what you forgot.

Did you overlook . . .

- training costs to bring team members up to speed?

- training costs at the back end to teach users to implement your project?

- ongoing personnel costs?

- ongoing maintenance costs for new spaces?

- costs for insurance?

- licensing fees?

- costs for outside support such as legal or accounting?

"Fully fund a project or do not start it."
    —Norman R. Augustine,
        former chairman and CEO, Lockheed Martin

A budget, no matter how carefully planned, is still just your best guess. Be prepared for actual numbers to deviate from your original estimates, and stay as flexible as possible within your limitations of time, quality demands, and total money available.

"[Say] a project comes from marketing. They get detailed input from the financial folks and the techno-geeks. They answer the rigorous financial questions, the capital stuff over time, the expenses, the headcount, the revenue. And these cross-functional teams make the plan look as good as it can look. Can I tell that it will succeed? There's due diligence, but it still could fail—or it might be more successful than you ever dreamed. It's the future and you still don't know."
    —Timothy O'Meara

Tip: If you work for a consulting or services firm such as an architectural company or ad agency, you and your client may have different assumptions about how flexible a budget can be. Avoid misunderstandings down the line by clarifying your perceptions of what a budget is early on.

What You COULD Do.

Let's return to Brett's problem.

The mentor suggests this solution:

Brett probably feels as though he is leading the project from hell. He will continue to feel this way unless he can bring some goals, organization, and structure to the project. He needs to meet immediately with all of the stakeholders of the project (not just his boss) and determine what they want the project to accomplish. Then he needs to meet with his project team and develop a concrete plan that includes milestones, key deliverables, priorities, and so on. Even if his team resists, Brett needs to engage them in creating a WBS that truly reflects the goals and activities of the project. Once the WBS is completed, the group needs to determine who will do what and when it will be done. He needs to break the cycle of the group delegating to him and plan for the project as a whole.

How to Manage
the Project

"A project manager needs the motivation of an optimist and the caution of a pessimist."

—Anne Briggs, product director

Putting the plan into action is the beginning of the implementation phase. For many project managers, this is the most enjoyable part of the job because the work is actually getting done—progress can be seen. But this phase can also be the most frustrating because the details can seem tedious and, at times, even overwhelming. Staying on top of these details is essential, however, so that you can enjoy the rest of the process.

Stay on the critical path

Once you're moving along the path from start to finish, make sure you stay on the critical path, even though at times it may not seem to be the straightest path.

"By critical path, I mean the shortest distance between the project's start and the finish line. Unfortunately, many people on the critical path—namely, project managers and development teams—see this path as the only route. But the path from start to finish is flexible—shortcuts and bushwhacking are usually feasible."

—Martin Nemzow

Be prepared to delegate

"Fifteen percent of the budget on a classroom building was for audiovisual wiring and equipment. I just couldn't keep up with it. It's a whole discipline in and of itself, and it's a rapidly changing field. I delegated that job to one person on the team. That's along with having hired an AV consultant! But I had to delegate that piece or I couldn't have run the job."

—Victor Ortale

Effective project managers spend up-front time planning work assignments and organizing resources to achieve business goals in the most productive way possible. Part of this process occurs when you assemble your team and assign responsibilities to each team member.

As the project proceeds, however, you may find that you need to delegate more tasks than originally anticipated. Be flexible enough to recognize the need to delegate tasks or functions whenever necessary.

Remember, though, that as project manager you have the final responsibility and are accountable for the overall project, so don't delegate tasks that *only you* can perform.

Deciding what (and what not) to delegate. First, determine which tasks you want to delegate, and what skills and capabilities will be required in order to complete each assignment successfully. Then, match the assignment with the most appropriate member of the team.

Delegate—and then trust your team members. Once you've decided how you will assign tasks to team members, give each person the information and resources needed to succeed. Then back off and let your team members do their jobs.

Monitor the project's progress

"Every project has milestones along the critical path. Milestones are, simply put, the points at which something should have been accomplished, with dire consequences if it hasn't been. The responsibility for meeting milestones may be someone else's, but the failure to meet them reflects badly on you and your team. As project manager, you are accountable for failures in a project even if you didn't cause them."

—Martin Nemzow

Whether you have a formal project control system in place or you do your own regular checking up on progress, try to maintain a big-picture perspective so that you don't become engulfed by details and petty problems.

Choose the right monitoring system for you and your project. No single monitoring system works for all projects. A system that's right for a large project can easily swamp a small one with paperwork, whereas a system that works for small projects won't have enough muscle for a big one.

Depending on the size and complexity of your project, you may want to use a system that you've developed through experience and feel comfortable with. But for larger projects, you'll probably need to install a project-monitoring software system. There are many different types of software programs available. You'll have to do some research and make inquiries before you make a decision about which one to implement.

Focus on what's important. When you find yourself immersed in the details of a project, it's easy to be diverted from the critical path to a side path that wastes your time. Keep asking yourself the following questions:

- What is important to the success of the project?

- What are we attempting to do?

- Which parts of the project are the most critical to track and control?

- What are the essential points at which controls need to be placed?

Emphasize timely information. You need to receive information in a reasonably fast manner for your responses to do any good at all. The best-case scenario is to get information on a real-time basis. In most cases, though, weekly updates will be fine.

Enable corrective action. Be responsive to changes in data or information. You need to be alert to early signs of problems. Be prepared to initiate corrective action; otherwise, all you are doing is monitoring, not exercising control. But be careful not to jump in too quickly—allow your team members to work out small problems on their own.

Monitor the project's budget

One of the most important responsibilities of a project manager is monitoring the budget. You've planned the project carefully; now you need to watch the numbers to ensure that real costs are matching the budgeted amounts. It's often difficult to predict future costs with complete accuracy, but you do need to have your project stay within the overall budgeted limits—or be ready to explain why extra costs are unavoidable.

When monitoring actual costs against your estimates, watch out for these common contingencies that can send your project over budget:

- unexpected inflation during long-term projects

- failure to factor in currency exchange rates or to predict unexpected fluctuations in exchange rates

- not getting firm prices from suppliers and subcontractors

- estimates based on different costing methods; for example, hours versus dollars

- unplanned personnel costs used to keep project on schedule, including increased overtime

- unexpected space needs

- unexpected training costs

- consultant fees to resolve unforeseen problems

Most of these contingencies could not have been predicted before the project began. That's why you need to stay alert to the real numbers as they come in. Watch for significant deviations from the budgeted amounts. Then find out the reason for the differences.

Tips: Choosing What to Delegate

- Assess your own workload and identify those tasks or functions that require your specific set of skills and authority.

- Identify routine tasks, specific activities, or complete functions that could easily be done by other team members or outside resources.

- Identify those tasks or functions that could be completed by team members if additional training or coaching were provided by yourself or one of your peers.

- Identify tasks or functions that may require expertise or skills from outside your department or organization.

Not all budget news is bad. When you monitor your budget against real costs, you may find some more encouraging data emerging. The following are some of the contingencies that can contribute to costs being under budget:

- capital expenditures not made as planned

- interest rates lower than expected

- staff not allocated as planned

Tips: Delegating Effectively

- Recognize the capabilities of your team.
- Trust your team's ability to get the job done.
- Focus on results—let go of your need to get involved in how tasks are accomplished.
- Consider delegation as a way to develop the skills of your team.
- Always delegate to the lowest possible level to make the best use of staff resources.
- Explain assignments clearly and provide resources needed for successful completion.
- Deflect reverse delegation—do not automatically solve problems or make decisions for your staff members. Focus on generating alternatives together.

"In video production, it never goes as planned, so you have to learn to roll with it. For a long time I wanted to control everything, and it was very hard and very frustrating. Once I accepted that there are things that are out of my control, I could deal with it. I can't control weather; I can't control really bad acne on an actor. Now if something happens, I get out of the 'blame' mode and get into the 'fix' mode. Now I ask, 'How we can solve the problem?' because the bottom line is I'm running a million-dollar

music video and it's going to get made one way or the other. Getting angry or upset doesn't help."

—Jennifer Sargent

Ensure quality control

Quality assurance also plays a major role in the success of any project. The last thing a project manager needs is a client, customer, supervisor, or other stakeholder who is dissatisfied with the end result.

A few guidelines can help you achieve high-quality products and results:

- Don't rush quality checks to meet deadlines. The cost of fixing problems after the fact is usually far greater than the cost of confronting and solving problems before they spin out of control.

- Determine quality benchmarks in the planning phase. Take into account things such as the quality policy of the organization, stakeholder requirements, the scope of the project, and any external regulations or rules.

- Inspect deliverables using the most appropriate tools, for example, detailed inspections, checklists, or statistical sampling.

- Accept or reject deliverables based on previously defined measures. Rejected deliverables can be returned or reworked, depending on costs.

Report progress to stakeholders

Communicating the project's progress to the stakeholders is another critical part of the project manager's job. Agree in the planning phase how and when you will present your reports.

"The biggest pitfall is not communicating clearly with your client. With some clients, you have to call and say that you sent the e-mail. And always take notes, even when you're having casual phone calls so you can track what was agreed upon, what is left outstanding, and who's responsible, so you can follow up on it."
—Beth Chapman

Establish a sound stakeholder communication system. Stakeholders generally want continuous updates, and project status and progress reports. Know what they want and keep them informed. As the project progresses, consult with stakeholders to see if the amount of information is sufficient and the format of the information useful. Your journey down the critical path will be smoother without unhappy stakeholders demanding more information.

Be honest. Don't hide or downplay problems as they come up, or you can easily transform a problem into a crisis—one that is twice as big as it would have been if you had alerted stakeholders to the difficulty in the first place. If you've kept them informed, they may even turn out to be resources, offering help when problems do arise.

"Once a project starts, it becomes organic. It gets extremely intense. If you thought you could plan for everything, you should probably be locked up. You have to be aware, attuned to what's happening, what's changing—and part of that is being obsessive, being on top of the details. You have to be aware of change so you can utilize whatever it is that just changed, because it might be an opportunity. And you have to monitor change so you can avoid risk downstream."

—Timothy O'Meara

How to Manage
the Problems

"Focus on the problem, not on fault-finding."

—Anonymous

One of the exciting aspects of project management is dealing with the unexpected. Most surprises can be handled quickly and effectively. Too often, however, a project manager is confronted with problems that can threaten the very success of the project.

Manage "mission creep"

In addition to unpredictable change, project managers often face internal pressure to change the scope of the project. When stakeholders ask for changes, it's your job to communicate clearly to them how these changes will affect the cost, time, or quality of the project.

On some projects, "mission creep" is an ongoing battle for the project manager. (In software circles, this phenomenon is sometimes called "feature creep.") After specific milestones and budgets have been agreed upon, people may begin to see more that could be achieved. Don't get caught up in trying to solve problems that lie beyond the established scope of your project—even problems that your company urgently needs to address.

"When your client wants something unreasonable, you have to keep your sense of humor. You spell out the consequences, make the alternatives really clear. You've got to have common sense. I'm always saying in meetings, does it really make sense to do this?"

—Victor Ortale

Manage the time slippage problem

The most common problem in project management is when a project begins to fall behind schedule. Delays may be unavoidable, but more often than not there are actions you can take to remedy—or at least improve—the situation. The first step is to recognize the problem. If you've been monitoring the project's progress carefully, you'll quickly notice when schedules are being readjusted to accommodate delays or unexpected bottlenecks.

Manage the people problems

Some project managers tend to ignore potential people problems during the planning phase, and, even when these problems become real and evident, they may still deny or avoid them. Unfortunately, people problems are often the most difficult challenges a project manager has to confront. So, rather than ignoring, denying, or trying to avoid them, be prepared for people problems—and act quickly to solve them.

Remember: Not all types of people problems are the same or require the same action. Here's how to recognize and deal with some of the different situations you'll encounter.

What Would YOU Do?

The Best-Laid Plans

Last year, the holiday season was not a happy one for Randy. When Bright Light, Inc., failed to deliver a key part, the whole Tyranna-Bot project had come to a grinding halt. The only Tyranna-Bots to hit the market in time had been drawn from existing stock. This time, Randy found a more reliable vendor and built extra time into the schedule, yet here he was, facing another disaster. The chips that made Megala-Bot talk were defective. The supplier was scrambling for more, but there would be another serious delay, and the extra time in the schedule wouldn't cover it. Randy didn't want to stop the project, as he had last time, but how could he keep the job on schedule? The advertising blitz was underway and customers were waiting for their Megala-Bots. Randy did not want to disappoint them—or his boss!

What would YOU do? The mentor will suggest a solution in *What you COULD do.*

Tips: Controlling Project Slowdowns

Try these approaches before accepting the inevitability of a delay in project completion:

- Renegotiate. Discuss with stakeholders about increasing the budget or extending the deadline.
- Use later steps to recover. Reexamine budgets and schedules to see if you can you make up the time elsewhere.
- Narrow project scope. Are there nonessential elements of the project that can be dropped to reduce costs and save time?
- Deploy more resources. Can you put more people or machines to work? Weigh the costs against the importance of the deadline.
- Accept substitution. Can you substitute a less expensive or more readily available item?
- Seek alternative sources. Can another source supply the missing item?
- Accept partial delivery. Can you accept fewer of an item to keep work going, and complete the delivery later?
- Offer incentives. Can you offer bonuses or other incentives for on-time delivery?
- Demand compliance. Will demanding that people do what they said they would get the desired result? This may require support from upper management.

In general, these people problems can be avoided or handled early on if you, as project manager, communicate frequently with each team member. Weekly staff meetings may not be enough; daily communication—with individual team members and with the team as a whole—may be necessary.

"The project manager has to manage both the tasks and the people. Typical project management training is about the task, but the reality is that where people really feel challenged is on the people side."
—Mary Grace Duffy, management consultant

Pay attention to the small signs of emerging problems, such as a team member's

- increased tension and irritability,

- loss of enthusiasm for job,

- restlessness and pacing, or

- inability to make decisions.

When you see the first signs of a problem, deal with it quickly. Don't let it grow from a small irritant into a major crisis.

?What You COULD Do.

Remember Randy's dilemma?

Here's what the mentor suggests:

This may be a case of Murphy's Law prevailing—that no matter what Randy does, he may not get sufficient product to market for the holidays. However, he has to give it his best shot. In this case that probably means scouting for other vendors, paying more for extra production runs, and lining up last-minute distribution channels. He also needs to review his critical path to determine if any adjustments in sequence can be made; for example, can packaging be prepared prior to the receipt of the finished Megala-Bot rather than waiting until after delivery of the product?

Team Structure Problems

Problem	Possible Causes	Potential Impact	Recommended Action
Lack of skills/ missing skills	• Certain skills overlooked during planning. • Need for new skills discovered in the midst of the project.	The project will not move forward as fast as it should, or might be stalled.	• Arrange for a team member to be trained in the skills needed. • Hire outside consultants or contractors who have the required skills.

continued

Problem	Possible Causes	Potential Impact	Recommended Action
Team member leaves	There are many reasons why a team member might leave the project.	The severity of the impact depends on the skills and knowledge that are lost with the person: • If the work can be easily redistributed or another person with the same skills and expertise can be quickly hired, then the impact may be slight. • If not, then the loss could create a crisis.	• Consider having backups for critical skills. • Cross-train team members so that they can fill in for one another. • Make the departure of one person an opportunity to bring on board an even more skilled member.

Interpersonal Problems

Problem	Possible Causes	Potential Impact	Recommended Action
Team members are too friendly	Team members spend excessive amounts of time chatting and discussing personal problems.	• Decreased overall productivity. • Time is wasted and work on the project is slowed down. • Hard-working team members may resent those who work less efficiently.	• Emphasize that social gatherings need to be planned after work hours. • Reorganize team subgroups to disrupt the formation of cliques.

Problem	Possible Causes	Potential Impact	Recommended Action
Inflexible team members	• Team member may believe that their way is the only right way. • Team member may be anxious about trying new approaches.	• Team member may not keep up with colleagues. • Team member may block others' progress.	• Indicate goals and expectations at the start of the project. • Address the team member's concerns or fears. Try to work with him in moving toward change.
Conflicts within team	Many potential causes, including differences in working style, personalities, areas of expertise, and so on.	Conflicts can affect schedule, quality of work, overall productivity, and team cohesiveness.	• Focus on the project's goals, not personal feelings. • Be compassionate, but fair. • Separate the underlying causes from the surface disturbances. • Work on solutions, not blame.

Productivity Problems

Problem	Possible Causes	Potential Impact	Recommended Action
Time spent on wrong tasks	• Poor time management. • Team member prefers some tasks over others, regardless of relative importance. • Project manager may have sent the wrong message about task priorities.	• Work on critical tasks may be delayed. • Project may be delayed.	• Emphasize to team which tasks are most important. • Assign tasks to two team members to work on together. • Provide resources to help team member improve time-management skills.

continued

Problem	Possible Causes	Potential Impact	Recommended Action
Poor-quality work	• Team member misunderstands the requirements of the job. • Work is measured by different standards. • Team member does not have adequate skills to complete the task.	• Work may have to be redone, costing money and time. • The project may fail.	• Be clear from the start about the quality expectations and the standards of measure. • Develop an action plan for improving the quality of the team member's work. • Provide training and support for the person to develop his skills.
Burnout	• Team member is overcommitted to the project. • Team member is taking on too many tasks or activities, both at work and beyond work. • Team member works too long at one type of task.	• Productivity may decline. • Team member may not be able to continue to work at all.	• Encourage the team member to take a break or a vacation to gain fresh energy. • Help the team member to readjust her work schedule or work level.

How to Handle
End Matters

> *"At the conclusion of the job, the big reward to me
> is actualizing and coming in under budget."*
> —Jennifer Sargent

The final stage in the life cycle of a project is the phase-out, during which your team completes its work. If all went as planned—the tasks fulfilled, the problems solved, the stakeholders satisfied—then congratulate yourself and your team. It's a time for celebration.

If, as is more likely, there were some rough spots along the way—the project took longer than expected; the result was less than hoped for, or the actual cost was underestimated—it's still important to recognize the team's efforts and accomplishments.

In either case, before the team moves on to other projects or breaks up and parts company, make sure you have scheduled time to debrief and document the process so that the full benefit of "lessons learned" can be shared.

"The satisfaction I get from project management is seeing the end product. When the building is done and people like it, you're responsible for having gotten it there, despite all the odds, the poor planning, and the wacko client."
> —Victor Ortale

Perform a post-project evaluation

The purpose of the post-project evaluation is to bring your team together for one last meeting in order to identify (1) what went well and (2) what went wrong. Make a list of "best practices" to help future projects go more smoothly, and discuss how to improve the process and avoid problems during the next project.

Encourage a spirit of learning. Use the evaluation as an opportunity to learn, not as a time to criticize and blame. If some team members fear they'll be punished for past problems, they may try to hide those problems rather than help to find better ways of handling them in the future.

Bring in outside facilitators. Project evaluations are best conducted by an independent person who can objectively assess the information. Typically, the individual team members have been working so closely with each other they have lost some perspective on the process. An independent facilitator can sort out the emotional from the practical issues.

One example of a post-evaluation report is shown on page 77.

Develop a useful final report

The final report documents all information that will be useful not only for the current project manager, team members, and stakeholders, but for future project managers who may use the information to plan their own projects.

A typical post-project evaluation report includes the following:

- **Current project status:** What were the original objectives, and what has been achieved?

- **Future status:** What will happen to the project now that it has been completed? Will it be incorporated into an ongoing production process; was it part of a larger project, or was it a self-contained entity that has completed its goals?

- **Status of ongoing critical tasks:** What is the current condition of ongoing tasks that contain either a high level of technical risk or are being performed by outside vendors or subcontractors, over whom the project manager may have limited control?

- **Risk assessment:** Are there, or were there, any risks that could have a potential for financial loss, project failure, or other liabilities?

- **Information relevant to other projects:** What were the lessons learned that can be applied to other projects either under way or being planned?

- **Limitations of the audit:** Are there any factors that might limit the validity of the audit? Are there assumptions that could be changed or information that is missing or suspect? Did anyone in the group or team seem to resist providing complete information?

PROJECT MANAGEMENT TOOLS

Project Phase-Out Analysis and Lessons Learned

Project name:	Project Phoenix		Date: 5/29/200X
Present at this session:	Rafael, Phil, and Carmen		

Project Phase/Task	What Worked	What Didn't Work	Ways to Improve
Equipment acquisition	Obtained the Web servers on time and on budget.	Logistical problems with availability of database servers—caused a delay. Expedited order that introduced additional expense.	Need to order equipment earlier.
Provision and implement equipment	Two days were recovered through the efforts of Rafael and Carmen during provisioning phase.		
Test Equipment	Testing phase was successful; during testing, a bug in the database content was discovered and corrected prior to cutover.		
Go live with new equipment	Smooth cutover with minimal downtime.	Some users were unaware that there would be a brief outage.	Publicize work window to user base more aggressively.
Test again	Tested fine.		
Decommission old equipment	Decommissioned sites and erased content successfully; reabsorbed stock into inventory.	Some confusion over serial numbers and inventory, but straightened out in the end.	Check serial numbers at an earlier phase to minimize problems at the end of project.

Target analysis: How well did the project/team do ...

In achieving goals and meeting project objectives?
Success; all goals were achieved.

At meeting deadlines and the final completion date?
Success; met our target date.

At monitoring and staying within budget?
Success; we were well within projected budget parameters.

At communicating with stakeholders?
Partial success; we could have done better at communicating requirements earlier to individuals involved in the phases of the project.

Resources assessment: Were the resources allocated appropriate, sufficient and efficiently used? *(i.e., time, people, money)*

Generally, the resource allocations were appropriate. The project went slightly over budget, but was not inappropriate. The people involved had the expertise necessary to carry out the highly technical phases of the project. The time resources were appropriate as the project was completed on time with no room to spare.

Lessons learned: What are the key lessons learned that can be applied to future projects?

At each phase of the project, it is crucial to anticipate the next steps and to alert groups or individuals of resource requirements as early as possible in the process. By so doing, we probably could have acquired the equipment in a more timely manner and would not have had to scrabble so much in the latter phases to meet our target dates.

Enjoy the satisfaction
of a job well done

Take a moment to look back at the entire process. Acknowledge the bumps experienced in the journey, but mark the conclusion with good cheer and some relief.

Tips and Tools

Tools for
Project Management

Defining Your Project

Uncover the issues and parameters at the core of your project.

The "Real" Project

What is the perceived need or purpose for what we are trying to do?

What caused people to see this as a problem that needed solving?

What criteria are people going to use to judge this project a success?

The Stakeholders

Who has a stake in the solution or outcome?

How do the various stakeholders' goals for the project differ?

What functions or people might the project's activities or outcomes affect?

Who is going to contribute resources? (People, space, time, tools, money)

Skills Required for the Project

Skill Needed	Possible Team Member
1.	1.
2.	2.
3.	3.
4.	4.
5.	5.
6.	6.

Work Breakdown Structure

Develop a Work Breakdown Structure (WBS) to ensure that you do not overlook a significant part of a complex activity or underestimate the time and money needed to complete the work. Use multiple pages as needed.

Describe the overall project:

Major Task	Level 1 Sub Tasks	Level 2 Sub Tasks	Level 2 Sub Task Duration
Total Duration *(hours/weeks/days)*			

Major Task	Level 1 Sub Tasks	Level 2 Sub Tasks	Level 2 Sub Task Duration
Total Duration *(hours/weeks/days)*			

Project Progress Report

Use this form to help assess progress, present this information to others, and think through next steps.

Project:	Prepared by:

For the period from:	to:

Current Status

Key milestones for this period:

Achieved	Coming up next

Key issues or problems:

Resolved	Need to be resolved

Key decisions:

Made	Need to be made	By whom	When

Budget status:

Implications

Changes in objectives, timeline/delivery dates, project scope, resource allocation (including people and financial):

Next Steps

List the specific action steps that will be done to help move this project forward successfully.
Put a name and date next to each step if possible.

Step	Person Responsible	Date

Comments

Selecting Scheduling Software

Survey the options available, and the preferences and work habits of your team.
Use the comparison grid to evaluate project-planning software you may consider.

What's Worked Before

Seek recommendations from project members and other colleagues about what planning methods they have used.
Supplement with research from trade magazines and software vendors.

Pros and cons of recommendations?

Work habits of project members? Preferences for working with a particular method?

Rank the software packages being considered. Do they ...	Software Packages (0 = no, 1 = yes)		
	1	**2**	**3**
1. Handle development of and changes to Gantt charts and flow charts, including PERT diagrams and calculations of critical paths? *Notes*	☐	☐	☐
2. Produce schedules and budgets? *Notes*	☐	☐	☐
3. Integrate project schedules with a calendar allowing for weekends and holidays? *Notes*	☐	☐	☐
4. Create different scenarios for contingency planning and updating? *Notes*	☐	☐	☐
5. Check for overscheduling of individuals and groups? *Notes*	☐	☐	☐
6. Provide on-screen viewing of information before printing? *Notes*	☐	☐	☐
7. Generate the preprogrammed simple, readable reports you want? *Notes*	☐	☐	☐
8. Provide functionality to customize reports? *Notes*	☐	☐	☐
9. (Any team preferences in addition to above?) *Notes*	☐	☐	☐
Overall Rank:			

Project Phase-Out Analysis and Lessons Learned

Use this form with the project team to assess the project. Summarize the "lessons learned" for use in future projects.

Project name:	Date:
Prepared by:	

Present at this session:

For each major phase of the project (or key tasks), identify what worked (what we did right), what didn't work, and ways the team could improve the process the next time.

Project Phase/Task	What Worked	What Didn't Work	Ways to Improve

Target analysis: How well did the project/team do ...

In achieving goals and meeting project objectives?

At meeting deadlines and the final completion date?

At monitoring and staying within budget?

At communicating with stakeholders?

Resources assessment: Were the resources allocated appropriate, sufficient and efficiently used?
(i.e., time, people, money)

Lessons learned: What are the key lessons learned that can be applied to future projects?

Test Yourself

Test yourself offers ten multiple-choice questions to help you identify your baseline knowledge of project management.

Answers to the questions are given at the end of the test.

1. You've been assigned a project, and it appears to have explicit, set expectations and clearly outlined responsibilities. Before you begin planning, what should you do first?

    a. Ensure that the funding has been approved.

    b. Confirm that the project is solving the right problem.

2. Why is it critical to spend time early in the planning phase identifying all the stakeholders in your project's activities or outcomes?

    a. To find potential champions who will support the project.

    b. To ensure that the project objectives meet everyone's expectations of success.

    c. To be politically astute and identify possible obstacles early.

3. In the planning phase, you are advised to beware of "mission creep." What is "mission creep"?

    a. Mission creep is unwittingly giving in to pressure to do more than has originally been planned for.

    b. Mission creep is agreeing to extend the schedule without a corresponding increase in funding

4. When you are defining project objectives, what three variables most often determine what is possible for you to consider?

    a. Available resources, how realistic the project is, and time limits.

    b. Complexity, time, and resources.

    c. Time, cost, and quality.

5. What are you doing when you are creating a WBS analysis?

    a. You are subdividing the overall project into smaller tasks, and then subdividing the smaller tasks further until you get to the desired task size.

    b. You are distributing the allocated funding across the project objectives, to consider and anticipate personnel and activity costs.

6. When assembling a team for your project, make sure you have a group

    a. who will get along with each other during the project.

    b. that is dedicated to success of the project.

    c. with all the skills needed for the project.

7. You need to track what has to be done, how long a particular activity will take, in what order it has to happen, and who is going to be responsible for it. Which project management tool will do this?

    a. WBS Analysis.

    b. Gantt or flow charts.

8. Complete the statement: "A budget is not only a list of all the costs involved in executing a project. It is also _____."

   a. a look at whether the project's benefits justify its costs

   b. a tracking tool that allows the manager to control implementation

   c. the tool that you as manager use to justify any future need for additional monies

9. When developing the project budget, which of the following variables is not one of the standard categories considered and, indeed, is frequently overlooked?

   a. Personnel.

   b. Travel.

   c. Supplies.

   d. Maintenance.

   e. Research/Training.

10. In the best of all possible worlds, who conducts the evaluation of a completed project?

   a. The project manager, with all stakeholders providing input.

   b. An independent person who can be objective.

   c. The individual(s) who identified the initial problem and project.

Answers to test questions

1, b. It is a good idea to confirm that the project will indeed meet the organization's underlying need. The expectations can be clear, yet still not go to the heart of the issue. Until you know the answers to underlying questions, you run the risk of wasting time and money on a project that is either too simplistic or too complicated.

2, b. You need to know exactly what success on the project means to people or departments who will be affected by the project's outcomes. One of your critical tasks in the planning phase is to meld stakeholders' expectations into a coherent and manageable set of project objectives.

3, a. Mission creep is unwittingly giving in to pressure to do more than has originally been planned for. As you find out each stakeholder's definition of success, you can get caught up in trying to solve problems beyond the scope of your project. Guard against giving in to pressures to expand the project's mission without ensuring that this is critical to a majority of stakeholders.

4, c. Time, cost, and quality are the three variables that most often determine your project objectives—change any one of these and you change your outcome. The reality is that the quality of the project result that is feasible depends heavily on the time and funding you have.

5, a. Using the WBS (Work Breakdown Structure), a complex activity is subdivided into smaller and smaller tasks until the activity can no longer be divided or you reach the task size you are looking for. The outcomes become the basis for developing estimates, assigning personnel, tracking progress, and showing the scope of project work.

6, b. A group needs to be committed to the project. The members may not always agree, but they have to trust that they are all working toward the same goal. A team is usually assembled according to its members' skills, but skills can also be gained through training—having all the skills required is not necessarily the top priority when assembling a productive team.

7, b. Both Gantt charts and flow charts are generally accepted methods of scheduling projects. Of the two approaches, use the method with which you are comfortable and familiar. There is no one right way to develop scheduling.

8, a. A look at whether the project's benefits justify its costs. When the budget amount is preset, it is important that the manager clarify for stakeholders how quality and budget are interrelated.

9, c. Maintenance is often forgotten. However, once a project is completed, there may be ongoing maintenance costs that need to be considered during budget development.

10, b. An independent auditor is the usually most objective evaluator. But even when an independent auditor is not available, the evaluation must be done in a spirit of learning, not with an attitude of criticism and blame.

To Learn More

Notes and Articles

Jeffrey Elton and Justin Roe. "Bringing Discipline to Project Management." *Harvard Business Review.* March–April 1998.

> The authors critique the application of Goldratt's theory of constraints to the realm of project management and provide advice for managing a portfolio of projects.

Jeffrey K. Pinto and Om P. Kharbanda. "How to Fail in Project Management (Without Really Trying)." *Business Horizons,* 1996.

> Project-management techniques have met with widespread acceptance as a means of expediting product development, making efficient use of resources, and stimulating cross-functional communication. Yet failures and outright disasters abound in the history of project management. A study of these failures indicates a dozen sure-fire methods for dooming a project, such as: ignore its environment; push a new technology to market too quickly; don't bother to build in fallback options; when problems occur, shoot the person most visible; and so on. However, past failure need not discourage us from future efforts. Indeed, it is through these past failures that we gain the savvy to push on to successful ventures.

"What You Can Learn from Professional Project Managers." *Harvard Management Update*, February 2001.

Companies that manage large capital projects or a multitude of simultaneous projects—manufacturing, engineering, and construction firms—have long recognized the need for expertise in the techniques of planning, scheduling, and controlling work. But over the past decade, non–project-driven firms—especially those that see themselves as selling solutions rather than products—have seen the light, too. As a result, project management has become increasingly important and complex. But even if you're not a certified project manager, you can still benefit from the professionalization of the field.

Books

H. Kent Bowen. *Project Management Manual*. Boston: Harvard Business School Publishing, 2001.

A descriptive manual of how to manage the process of project management. Major sections are: (1) define and organize the project, (2) plan the project, and (3) track and manage the project. Twelve processes are described in detail. Teaching purpose: To teach students that structured project planning is necessary for successful project outcome.

David I. Cleland. *A Guide to the Project Management Body of Knowledge*. Newtown Square, PA: Project Management Institute, 2000.

The Project Management Body of Knowledge (PMBOK®) is an inclusive term that describes the sum of knowledge within the profession of project management. The guide also provides a common lexicon for talking about project management. Project management is a relatively young profession, and while there is substantial commonality around what is done, there is relatively little commonality in the terms used. An extensive glossary further aids in standardizing definitions of the most important concepts, terms, and phrases.

Paul C. Dinsmore. *The AMA Handbook of Project Management.* New York: AMACOM, 1993.

This comprehensive handbook on project management is a source for project management techniques for both traditional and emerging industries. Presents critical concepts common to all projects, as well as in-depth solutions for specific areas such as change management, research and development, and international projects.

Marion E. Haynes. *Project Management: From Idea to Implementation.* Menlo Park, CA: Crisp Publications, Inc., 1996.

This step-by-step guide to project management is designed to help readers conceive, plan, implement, and evaluate any project from initial planning to finalization.

Peter G. W. Keen. *Every Manager's Guide to Business Processes: A Glossary of Key Terms and Processes for Today's Business Leader.* Boston: Harvard Business School Press, 1996.

Business processes comprise how work is coordinated, streamlined, and targeted to meet fundamental goals (e.g., customer service, time to market, and effective decision making). The book identifies and defines the key business process concepts and terms, highlighting what managers need to know to take effective action. The author's goal is to help managers sort reality from hype in the many claims of process movements, identify the most effective tools and techniques for process investment, and create a business process advantage for their firm.

Harold Kerzner. *Project Management: A Systems Approach to Planning, Scheduling, and Controlling,* 7th ed. New York: John Wiley, 2001.

Project management as a discipline grew out of the need during World War II for a system to manage the schedule, cost, and specifications of large multi-task projects. Since that time, it has largely been employed in the construction industry because of the large multi-task nature of civil and construction projects. Over the last decade, the use of project management techniques in general business methods (planning, scheduling, and controlling) has risen sharply.

James P. Lewis. *Fundamentals of Project Management.* WorkSmart Series. New York: AMACOM, 1995.

Based on best practices of experts in the field, this book explains how to set up project plans, schedule work effectively, establish priorities, monitor progress, and achieve performance objectives, while working faster and more profitably.

James P. Lewis. *Project Planning, Scheduling, and Control: A Hands-On Guide to Bringing Projects in On Time and On Budget.* New York: McGraw Hill, 1995.

> This application-oriented guide can be used to manage many different types of projects. Topics addressed include: how to decide if project management is needed; setting up the seven components of a project management system; applying the method of paired comparison to establish priorities and objectives; the eight areas for planning; and the project manager's role.

Vijay K. Verma. *Managing the Project Team.* The Human Aspects of Project Management series, vol. 3. Upper Darby, PA: Project Management Institute, 1997.

> This book focuses on developing and sustaining the project team. Promotes working interdependently in a climate of mutual trust and a win-win atmosphere.

Vijay K. Verma. *Organizing Projects for Success.* The Human Aspects of Project Management series, vol. 1. Upper Darby, PA: Project Management Institute, 1997.

> Covers project organization design, including understanding the issues of authority, accountability, reliability, and responsibility; effective delegation; interfacing with stakeholders; and making a matrix structure work.

Paul B. Williams. *Getting a Project Done on Time: Managing People, Time, and Results.* New York: AMACOM, 1996.

> This handy guide provides easy-to-read guidelines on all the essential project management skills. Provides easy-to-use tools, checklists, and tips.

Sources for
Managing Projects

We would like to acknowledge the sources that aided in developing this topic.

Norman R. Augustine, former chairman and CEO. Lockheed Martin.

Peter L. Baskette, supervisor. Genuity, Inc.

Ken, Bell, producer.

Anne Briggs, product director. Harvard Business School Publications.

Beth Chapman, engagement manager. Health Care Consulting Services Group, McKesson Corp.

Mary Grace Duffy, partner at the Cambridge Hill Partners, Cambridge, MA.

Susanna Erlikh, software development project manager. Rational Software Corp.

Matt Hotle, senior analyst. Gartner Group.

Martin Nemzow, high-tech consultant.

Timothy O'Meara, director of new and technical services. Ameritech Indiana.

Victor Ortale, project designer/project architect. Associate, Goody Clancy.

Jennifer Sargent, film and video producer.

H. Kent Bowen. *Project Management Manual*. Boston: Harvard Business School Publishing, 2001.

Paul C. Dinsmore. *The AMA Handbook of Project Management*. New York: AMACOM, 1993.

Jeffrey Elton and Justin Roe. "Bringing Discipline to Project Management." *Harvard Business Review*, March–April 1998.

Marion E. Haynes. *Project Management: From Idea to Implementation*. Menlo Park, CA: Crisp Publications, Inc. 1996.

James P. Lewis. *Fundamentals of Project Management*. WorkSmart Series. New York: AMACOM, 1995.

James P. Lewis. *Project Planning, Scheduling, and Control: A Hands-On Guide to Bringing Projects in On Time and On Budget*. Chicago: Probus Publishing Company, 1995.

Bennet P. Lientz and Kathryn P. Rea. *Breakthrough Technology Project Management*. San Diego: Academic Press, 1999.

Vijay K. Verma. *Organizing Projects for Success*. The Human Aspects of Project Management series, vol. 1. Upper Darby, PA: Project Management Institute, 1997.

Paul B. Williams. *Getting a Project Done on Time: Managing People, Time, and Results*. New York: AMACOM, 1996.

Notes

Notes

Notes

Notes

Notes

Notes

Notes

Notes

Notes

Notes

Notes

Notes

Notes

Notes

Notes

How to Order

Harvard Business School Press publications are available worldwide from your local bookseller or online retailer.

You can also call:
1-800-668-6780

Our product consultants are available to help you 8:00 a.m.–6:00 p.m., Monday–Friday, Eastern Time. Outside the U.S. and Canada, call: 617-783-7450.

Please call about special discounts for quantities greater than ten.

You can order online at:
www.HBSPress.org